Written by
Peter Jailall

Illustrated by
Shirley Aguinaldo

IOWI

Stop! Stop!
don't be a bully

written by Peter Jailall
illustrated and designed by Shirley Aguinaldo
published by In Our Words, Inc. / inourwords.ca

Library and Archives Canada Cataloguing in Publication

Jailall, Peter, author
Stop! Stop! don't be a bully / written by Peter Jailall;
illustrated by Shirley Aguinaldo.

Issued in print and electronic formats.
ISBN 978-1-926926-54-4 (paperback).--ISBN 978-1-926926-55-1 (pdf)

    1. Bullying--Juvenile poetry. I. Aguinaldo, Shirley, illustrator
II. Title.

PS8569.A414S76 2015   jC811'.54   C2015-906001-X

                                            C2015-906002-8

Dedication

*(for Aylan Kurdi, 3-year-old Syrian child refugee
washed ashore in Turkey)*

STOP the war!
Think about the little boy
wearing blue and red
looking for a place
to lay his head.

STOP!
It doesn't matter
His colour, creed or nationality
He belongs to the human family.

STOP!
Think about his journey!
A refugee searching
For a country...
A castaway at sea
Looking for a peaceful
place to be...

Stop! Stop!
Don't call me *Eskimo!*

I'm *First Nations,* living far
in the deep white snow.

Stop! Stop!
Don't call me black!
I can't go back.

Stop! Stop!
Don't call me white!
That's not right.

Stop! Stop!
Don't call me brown!
I've always been around.

Stop! Stop!
I may be just off the plane
But I do have a name.

Stop! Stop!
Don't call me gay...
I hear what you say.

Stop! Stop!
Don't call me a dummy!
That's not funny.

What if someone were to say
Mean things to YOU one day?

Stop! Stop!
Don't make fun of what I wear!
It's not nice to point and stare.

Stop! Stop!
Don't call me poor!
Sometimes less is more!

Stop! Stop!
Don't make fun of my walk
Or the way I talk.

Stop! Stop! Don't bully me
I have feelings too
Just like you

First Nations, black, brown, white,
chubby or gay
We're all right in our own way.

CPSIA information can be obtained
at www.ICGtesting.com
Printed in the USA
LVIC04n0755081216
516321LV00001B/1